NOW WE DRINK ALONE IN THE DARK

poems by

Matthew DeGroat

Finishing Line Press
Georgetown, Kentucky

NOW WE DRINK ALONE IN THE DARK

This book is dedicated to the city of Edinburgh.

Copyright © 2024 by Matthew DeGroat
ISBN 979-8-88838-757-3 First Edition
All rights reserved under International and Pan-American Copyright Conventions. No part of this book may be reproduced in any manner whatsoever without written permission from the publisher, except in the case of brief quotations embodied in critical articles and reviews.

ACKNOWLEDGMENTS

Big thanks to the editors for first publishing the following;

"Sales Calls From Earth"—Iconoclast Magazine, 2023
"Art"—Cultural Daily, 2022
"Los Phobos"—Cultural Daily, 2022
"Ready To Die? Click Here!"—Pom Pom Press, 2022
"Guns"—New Note Poetry, 2022
"How To Go Viral On Tik Tok"—Oprelle Publications, 2022
"Itsemurha"—Gl.ork, (UK) 2023
"You Should Probably Date Me"—Jack Grapes Finalist, 2021
"Queen Victoria"—Cultural Daily, 2022
"Le Bowling"—Ethel Zine, 2023
"Going Down"—Bullshit Lit, 2023
"Words From The Beehive"—Wergle Flomp Finalist, 2021
"Scenes From The Local Cafe"—Poetry Cove (UK), 2022

Special Thanks to Alexis Rhone Fancher, Jerry T. Johnson, Matt Proctor, Charlie Anderson, Watershed Studios, Vanha Paukku, and to my Mother for being a constant inspiration.

Publisher: Leah Huete de Maines
Editor: Christen Kincaid
Cover Art: Matthew DeGroat
Author Photo: Matthew DeGroat
Cover Design: Elizabeth Maines McCleavy

Order online: www.finishinglinepress.com
also available on amazon.com

Author inquiries and mail orders:
Finishing Line Press
PO Box 1626
Georgetown, Kentucky 40324
USA

Contents

i. void / pathos

Van Goghing 1
Down By The Water 2
Sales Calls From Earth 4
Curriculum Vitae 5
Art 6
Los Phobos 7
Six American Poets 8
The Ghost Of Hank Chinaski 9
Keys Wallet Phone 11
Abortions 13
Ready To Die? Click Here! 14
Odottaa 16
Guns 17
All The Way Home 18
How To Go Viral On TikTok 20
Psychic 21
Posthumous Men 22
Urgent Care 24
Three Poems 25
Come On Collapse 26
Reverse Psychology 27
Time 29
Guitar 30
Untitled 99 32

ii. voyage / path(s)

History Repeats Itself 33
London Morning 34
Itsemurha 35
Pigeon 36
Budapest 37
Doctors Are Dead 38
Mr. November 39
Vienna 40
Sounds and Images From The Cottage Cafe 41
Tallinn 42
I Recommend Agriculture 44
Outside and Drunk Screaming at the Constellations 45

Bratislava 46
Havana 47
Baltic Jam 48
Death Sharp Minor 49
James Joyce's Cane 50
Algebra...51
Words...52
I've Never Been a Poet in Edinburgh 53
Halu 54
Pigeon Two 55
Timeless Junk Of The Soul..56
New York, Pt I 60
The Coda...61

iii. **passion / void**

School Of Eyes 63
You Should Probably Date Me..64
The Show Me State 65
Memorial Day 67
Confessions Of An Anti-Natalist 68
April Fools 69
Queen Victoria 70
OMFG..71
You Wish You Knew George 72
Le Bowling 74
Achtung!..76
A Poet's Critique 77
Going Down 78
Teenager..79
Carousel..80
Three Rings 81
Coke Zero Carbon 82
Something Happened On The Way To Poland.....................................83
The Bubble 84
Words From The Beehive 86
Tonight, I Should Have Been Laughing...88
Restart..89
Scenes From The Local Cafe 90

i. void/pathos

Van Goghing

i'll continue to drink
but i've quit laughing
              longing
to ingest the waters of
the edges of
your tongue
i can only write
when i should be sleeping or
like poetry should be,
—a half dream   state
and when i wake from this
        twisted and
cacophonous night
-mare without so much as
a corpse beside me
you'll know why i disappeared
you'll know why i went
hunting for
  a re-birth
a fresh start so still and quiet
i will have left behind
        my ears
in a box
underneath my love
-stained pillow

Down By The Water

the mets won that night
and i don't follow sports
and trans is trending
in america mix
my mortal enemies
        inside my guts
i feel the darkest sadness

the coldest light

i have ever felt
i take a sip of icy domestic
        penny whip
then she approaches me
        and backs away
           sometimes i feel
like i'm in a Scorsese film

cream cheese plaster
of paris bagels etc

i'm alone
and i'm wet and
i watch her hands   speak
i wish she would look over here
it's still midtown now
        it's still—
i wish she would look
        over here at me
away from the muscle man
dear mexican chef scrubs the grill
like nails on greasy greasy chalkboard
        like my reality interpreter
        drunk again behind the eyes
i'm nauseous and
it's sunday morning
              it's easy
  how can she
how can she keep
talking to him
 she's Picasso
  and he's rocks

       pretty pretty lesbians
through their smiley smiley
                  cocktail
straws
no bartender please just the check and
     hold
            my
    arms

she's outside smoking now
where i should be
i know her how do i know her
i step outside and pass her name
softly through my teeth
stranger danger—
you have this
       you have this
wonderful habit
of crashing

     into my life
             every time i hit
the very bottom of it

            sometimes i feel
like i'm in a Scorsese film
mummified alive and only

just trying

     to find my way home.

Sales Calls From Earth

just try and remember
you brought me here
against my will

i never asked to be born;

imagine for a moment that communication was possible
with me pre-conception. you would call up and you would say hey just i wanted to tell you
about a great opportunity and you'd explain to me how i'd be born and then molded and made to suffer and not only that but i would have to go to work for someone to earn money to pay for my suffering; to pay for things that grow in abundance, for free, things i would need in order to sustain life. and so on and so on and
        trump and cancer and so on.

and the beautiful woman next to me would say who is that calling and i'd place the palm of my hand over the receiver and look at her and say it's just another one of those goddamned sales calls from earth and she would say can't they ever take the hint? just fucking hang up!

and then i'd slide my hand off of the receiver and say into the phone, quite assertively, you know that is the most preposterous idea of an existence i have ever heard. i am one hundred percent not interested, please do not call here anymore.

and then i'd hang up

and the beautiful woman next to me would hand me a glass of single malt scotch and she'd say sounds like you dodged a bullet there and i'd suck down the whisky in one gulp and i'd look at her and say what the fuck is a bullet?

Curriculum Vitae

Name: Matthew
DOB: Night Owl
1111 27 1111

Synopsis Of My Existence:
I was born, under protest. music is paramount. then words. then skin and barley. I have never earned a decent salary thank you. death within thirty years. part-time smoker.

Objective: no spreadsheets. I am here to obey you. please, direct deposit.

Education: humans named eric. rock songs from the nineties. her fucking eyes art school and the picture of dorian gray.

Experience: 1996-2011, Rock Star at Earth
chain-smoked autographed skin blew lines and traveled erroneous pieces of land
       sorry father

2016—Present, Mid-Life Cantankerous divorcée
traveled the good bits of land slept with midlife crises and wrote copious amounts of fragments. double daily scotch and oh extreme lethargy when alone. death feels imminent. not mine necessarily but definitely someone's heart is either kaputt or krank (working on my Deutsch)
punctual time management team leader
                                skills

please do not contact me and

      references available upon request

Art

because you have to
because you piss and
bleed it
because you know
no other way
and would rather not
know an-other way
because suffering turns beautiful
and confessions into
songs
words become gospel
and dreams attainable

because you would rather *die*
than not have it at all

because you have to
because you must

because everything else besides that   drink

is completely
and utterly
meaning-less

Los Phobos

two whiskies two
high life please so
it's good to see you
how've you been?
your ongoing decay
is much more noticeable these days
I've been good
more contagious than less
contagious than
nineteen months of solitude
not loneliness mind you
solitude
and
not one single
honest suicide attempt

have you done much reading?
fornicated with
the television set evolution
debt abruptly saw you in the papers and
it's a damn shame it really really is and
personally I think you are innocent but maybe
look up at the stars tonight I mean really really look and
remember that
nothing. fucking. actually. matters.

take yer whisky shooters now
prost! cheers! sláinte!
raise your glass to the gods of nothing!
because in the end
all is
forgotten anyway
like ophiuchus or betamax
or like human kindness or
beautiful music
now all we know for certain
is that delta is here and
she's got me by the lungs
and that love and war
give birth
to fear and terror
respectively
read this
  in memory of me

Six American Poets

        pocket pocket kyoto osaka
thief of belts these negative hands
these rotting religions pickled new
testimonial be cool protect your
pavement gimme gimme six
american poets; 1. survivalist
jones 2. the girl with the feathers
3. tropical storm maria 4. oh doctor megan is
pretty fucking great 5. probably me and 6. that
captain pajamas—so now the heat
breaks onions bloom off the carpet's
topography though this is not
spring this is the antithesis this is
oscar wilde country this is fat
fat fat-land oh dairy oh dancer
or prancer on victim on murder
on climate on doomscroll c o l l i s i o n s
    between my eyelids
there dance premonitions only i
cannot tell you not here anyway so
be gone and be glorious
let your screen lights
shine

let your hearts be
updated automatically,
downloaded and
installed
        guts pumped
                full of
do-da-data 111

00101101 00
1010101000\
      101010
110
10
      100
101010101
\01

The Ghost Of Hank Chinaski

for Alexis

you summoned his ghost
i assume
perhaps with a Ouija board
like Che Guevara
on an acid trip
or maybe
it's just LA
and you knew other drunks
and poets who knew
       him
he would have liked
my work, you say

sometimes i catch myself in the mirror
i see an aging resemblance
i push my
thinning hair back with
a pair of dollar store
reading glasses
beer belly hangs
over my belt
cigarette in one hand
scotch in the other
women on the brain
art on the fingertips
Bach dominates the radio

in bed til noon,
i see a sad resemblance
but reading this now
made my day
this email is
one of your finest works
in my opinion
you brought
his pitiful ghost
into the present
into a sentence of words
including "my work"
today i will be a little less

dejected, deterred

today i will write and
drink
in his honor
        and yours

Keys Wallet Phone

ok got my
keys

check
        wallet check
sanitizer phone
                  kn95
check check
book paper pen
blister lower back
spasm check

chargers chargers carpal
       tunnel syndrome check
              comfort chronic
depression oh
here's my anxiety too ok
is that everything no my
cigarettes my lighter
crippling debt   ok keys right ok

lock up and go

check pockets
full bag full
                stomach full of

dizzying mind-scars
1.   father's second marriage-check
2.   middle school high school beatings
3.   republicans car wreck car crash mountainside
4.   murder girl belgium baby mama dies times ninety nine
5.   college vodka cheater cheater broken hearts
and fires and fires and fires and check

fuck   this bag
       is getting heavy shoulders neck better
              grab the ibuprofen ibuprofen check
america check the mta the
sea levels and
congress check

ok wait did i grab the cigarettes or

just the lighter wait—i
 death   ok
breathe just
turn around now
turn a-round and just
go back go

   back   inside

   and check

Abortions

i'm happy they finally
banned abortions
i mean what took
      so long
was tired of hearing that
any old teenager could just walk
                          into
a walmart and buy
a semi-
automatic abortion
and
      take it to school and
eliminate dozens in seconds

or how the police could just
pull out their abortions and
shoot any unarmed black man that
made untimely eye contact

these abortions have plagued us for too long

maybe we can turn a corner now
maybe this country will no longer be
the stage four cancer of the earth
we can be safer happier lighter live
longer

i can ride the train at night and
not have to worry that
someone in my car might be
carrying a concealed
and loaded   abortion
thank white jesus above
for this court
born and birthed
lucid enough
to finally ban
      these
wretched
                  abortions

Ready To Die? Click Here!

caution do not use
if zeal is broken
objects in terror
closure then it may appear
destruction of this product is
strictly encouraged to
extinction of a species
(human) may be best
followed by a meal
please do not impregnate
                      a nurse
if you are nursing
or pregnant
read obstructions carefully
only digest once chewed
thoroughly (ages 1 and up)
do not cooperate with
heavy machinery
do not collect go
do not enter this establishment
without a face
and / or proof
of fascination
elevate your eggs
do not masturbate
three to five hours before bed
eat standing up
drink only while laughing
change coconut oil
every four thousand meals
or if you can read this
now featuring non-toxic
choke-resistant terms
and conditions please read and
initial here:

                                  here:

   and here:
please insert your
epitaph now

too weak

      not quite
must be stronger !!!
      (try adding a capital letter)
—select all stoplights—

…thank you,
your epitaph has been registered
    do not attempt to prematurely
    escape this existence
*void where prohibited
do not leave your home if the following symptoms
persist
the number you've dialed is
all of a circus and currently busy
life out of range
please dry your car again later
    this poem will now

self-destruct.

Odottaa

staring into the void
the mind control
          device
i wonder how close
your fingertips are
to bringing the sun
back into my grey and
lifeless corpse
- translations of beauty
- interpretations of dying

i recall once having enough
          love to fill
- the oceans
- the canyons
- all the nothingness in god's queer universe

but i drowned   them all
flushed into oblivion
rushing onto the next stone
and the next stone
    and now

'just me and whisky again'
i spew out in a jocular manner
          but really
waitingwaitingwaiting
arms stretched out shaking pissing
and one question lingers
    like a birthday hangover;
frightened into frequencies
    and horrors
        i can no longer translate

Guns

guns guns guns
guns
guns guns guns guns
      guns guns
guns guns
guns guns;
  gunsgunsguns

guns guns / guns
guns
guns guns
guns guns guns guns??
  (guns guns guns)

guns guns
guns guns guns
guns guns guns gunsssss
  guns guns
guns
guns gunsguns
gunsguns guns
guns
   guns guns
   guns
   guns.

guns guns guns guns

guns // guns.

All The Way Home

you wake
and drop to the floor
count pushups and
listen to the news

i roll out of bed
sigh "not again"
siphon coffee and
read schopenhauer

you go to work
for nine hours
for someone else who
pays you in feces
        i jerk off
have a shower and
a cigarette and
write poems until
it's acceptable
to switch over
to scotch whisky
        usually just before sunset
        earlier if it's overcast

you get home
shaking, in tears
cook yourself a meal
knees wobbling aching
you read some book club trash
and fall asleep in a puddle
of yourself
        i'm out
wandering the streets cold
the pubs the women
i've had enough but clearly i have not
i feel myself   shrivel

you dream of glass pyramids
and sex in outer space
of kissing the walls of
a padded white room

i've got two smokes left

my head begins to dizzy and sore

your right hip is bruised
from decades of slumber

i grab a dollar slice
with my last two dollars
and i drink and i choke
       laughing to myself
       thinking of us

ha ha ha
       all the way home

How To Go Viral On TikTok

turned and tossed lost years to coma
panic failing panic falling
watching time slide down mach two mach three
through sewn shut eyes the sandman has my throat again and

awake!

eating ether fever dream
ok hello midday haze
lung lung check breath
in
pain
minimal
now stand erect now wobble
wobble towards the toilet
rinse the slumber from my tongue
check reflection suck yer
guts in
radio coffee
glasses tablet
tablet smoke smoke
worry worry
tablet television takeaway cry
sleep sleep
choke sleep
sleep dream die
repeat
and worry and worry and worry and worry

but write this down
and read aloud
at least alone and
three times daily:

someday
something
completely
different
this way
will come

Psychic

i walked past a psychic on the way
home i should have gone in but
i had to pee so badly
my back teeth were floating anyway
what would she say anyway
"you're doomed sir , that will
be twenty dollars"
and then i'd argue with her that
that the sign on the door said ten
and i only have thirteen anyway
and she'd say "just give me the ten
but i told you so"

Posthumous Men

passionate and weak
like no other mistake
in the world
a grey hawk
a comic strip
a two band radio
alive with static
spewing new color
from the restless
underground
to the tops of
soggy clouds
      i cut my lip, alone
on a stressful night
and rotate and move round
the furniture
lest i tire of the shape
of my prison
cell
this is all to say
no, to war
and now, to everlasting
sleep and a drink
for a toast to the
new blurred border
      that divides
the great and
the forgotten
perhaps i am not
a timely man
perhaps it is my fate
to be understood
posthumously
my lip
it still bleeds
into the
dark isolation
and icy wind or
the memory of your

wine-washed breath
      as i cut my heart
on a heavy morning sun

and march toward
the odds
that are forever
        against me

Urgent Care

re: in delirium anonymity
hopeless causeway
of the summit of the stars
please don't go
i need you now more than ever
and so on in free verse
et cetera et cetera
wine is wine is wine
but you try bleeding
only after sundown
this tumultuous and
        rapid decline
like an amusement park
chock full of chainsaws
locked in and slack-jawed
this is my stage
        my spotlight
my one man show and
it's poignant and sad and
it reeks of nickel and copper
do this / that be / love somebody
spend no money lust pull
your epitaph from a hat and
shout it from the deepest
caverns of your heart
if you can stand up if
you can keep forging ahead
if you can follow me so far
        please contact your
    nearest
      healthcare provider

Three Poems

I

i sometimes don't
capitalize proper nouns
no one word is
more important
than another
except for maybe
        Paramount

II

a journey must begin
with a single step
and i have been
walking backwards
my entire
        life

III

if i pour another wine
i'll be drunk and it will feel
nice though it may not be the
thing to do but since when am i the
man who does the thing to do

Come On Collapse

ex-juggernaut
jackhammer
from the rooftops
      i spy
another day of
whisky consumed and
sunshine wasted
patterns of cold frost
blue with the sounds
of cavernous echo
my pockets full of holes
bleeding heart of
      stone
if sweet death is
just another place
do i still long for travel
to places i have never been
and wish to never return from?

Reverse Psychology

maybe in another life
i could be born
(if i must be born)
east of the atlantic
i open the window
and let the words fall
in the order of the wind
because it's monday
and i always try my best
to do nothing on mondays
maybe i'll write a little
smoke a handful of
cigarettes or do a small
load of laundry
but mostly
i just exist
and try and make sense of it
but lightly and between meals
sometimes i squeeze my
brain so tightly thinking
of ways to make some
money appear
to lessen the worry
of my days and nights
but usually that just leads me
back to writing
      my favourite distraction
or my thumbs are sore
from all the swiping
but i know you're there
there there
you
      are
my favourite distraction
lead me back to writing
lessen the worry
of my days and my nights
squeeze the money
from my brain
between meals
try and make sense of it or
just exist
together

smoking cigarettes
doing laundry on a
nothing-nothing monday
let the words fall
out the window
into the atlantic
and pray pray pray
 we are never
           born
again.

Time

there's a certain amount of time
that should not pass
between drinks
i've clocked it at
about twenty-eight minutes
i sit in the garden and pray
to dionysus
that she arrives with the wine
by ten to seven

Guitar; (I Used To Write Luv Songs)

i'm not quite sure
when it began
when you took all
of my money
or gave me the plague
or stripped me of
my dignity
my drive
to go on
you destroyed
my mind
my "soul"
my throat and
my hands
i could have gone
anywhere done
        anything

but i gave my life to *you*
and you gave me back
this
        living
                void

tonight i return
to the stage where
i was born
in nineteen ninety six
and i piss on the
monitors;
spit on the crowd

after all
the masses
the humans so
hearing-impaired
drowning in the same
main stream
maybe it was them

        all along
maybe

it wasn't *you*
        layers of
red and blue and sun
burst , oh maybe
you never doubted me.
you gave me all you had
as well

the masses
the humans so
hearing-impaired
drowning in the same
main
        stream

the songs exploded into
the world's womb
and miscarried upon
deaf ears
overexposure
and a global underwhelming
and dying
        attention span
while the precious
recycled
mediocrity rose and
gave birth to a
silence
of
ignorance but

i love you guitar
and goodbye

forever

Untitled 99

sex, candy and
cigarettes
and then there's me:
a glorified tragedy
the deadliest blaze
thousands of red flags
dead bodies and
mad   dancing figures

      repeatedly

           falling apart

this funeral
is not
fun
anymore

ii. voyage / path(s)

History Repeats Itself

my lolita
summer is here

and how i abhor this city
let me count you the ways
the broken rails
      the broken rails

the hollow skulls
the odious heat
         but
a glimmer of hope
as a young russian girl
pours me mexican beer
at an irish pub
in chinatown

      then i'm lost again

London Morning

there's people on the streets
at three thirty a.m.
oslo is still raging
     outside
i half expected
a ghost town after two
this could almost be new york
but the streets are clean
and the air is potable
and now seventy quid
          to get to an airline
who will most certainly
rape and ravage the inner
linings of my wallet
like railroad Bill said
on the bus to Glasgow
"next thing you know
they'll be charging you
for the toilet"
  and all this
just to experience
a baltic autumn
and the slightest chance
 of cleaner lungs
   a beating heart
     and the sunrise
        during wartime

Itsemurha

i got all dressed up for
              nobody at all
day two of the twilight
zone parade
counting statues
and holes in the sky
i walk beside myself
i've only heard certain
                  words
fall from the tongues
of the fewest of humans:
'fear of the god'
'of the dark side'
'this is suicide month'
i check my phone for the remedy,
watch the police
          forage rooftops,

          and i fail forward
my face warms the cool
misty air

pictures of world leaders
warm my heart no more

my tongue bleeds
          —i am alone here

zero connectivity
              perfect wanderlust

Pigeon

fucking pigeon
he doesn't know
of plague
or of debt

Budapest

hungarian doll
plucked fresh from the cult
of the church and
of the god
who hath forsaken you
stolen your family
loaded you with gravity
i am not this god
if things seem too heavy
allow me
to carry something
the burden of grief
heavier than the burden
        of plague
or at least here
in this city
where it feels like
the perfect marriage
of old times
        and end times
of sunshine
        and of fire
the river divides us
warmth bathes you in Pest
while i shiver in Buda
trembling in rainbows
it's long cold night
when you're terrified of walls
it's a long walk home
   when home is everywhere
      and nowhere all at once

Doctors Are Dead

there's nothing like
being propositioned
on the street by giggly sex
       workers
to remind a man
of his en-tombed
              loneliness
in a city full of couples
holding hands and
strolling the cobblestone
       though i suppose
i'm not completely alone
there was the Irish girl
who bummed a smoke and
the local man told me that
'all doctors are dead'
and there's Ukrainian mike who's always good
       for a joke or two
          no   i'm not alone
i sip my vodka across from
a girl who sits in a window
with a microphone pressed
to her lips giving me
her best time after time
it makes me shiver and
the tears buried within
dampen my dry throat
       and warm my icy
              jaded heart

Mr. November

november is always the same
every year
second hand coat
roll yer own smokes
                alone
find a woman who will have me
pay her four hundred euros on the first
for lodging and
fuck off elsewhere
before the thirtieth
it's cold but not cold enough
to be of any significant comfort
too much love or none at all
unusually longing for human heat
november holds no in-between
it takes no sides

friends crawl back to office spaces and
flights get cancelled
debt begins to slowly tighten its
grip around my throat
i follow the old man into the street
as my shadow screams
excuse me then
mr bouncer
where do the lonely november women
congregate in this town?
because i used to be attractive
maybe even charming
      for decades

but that fades with age
and with decay
        —with the wisdom of
    knowing the difference

Vienna

this fucker
on his phone
what an awful city
to be looking down in

Sounds And Images From The Cottage Cafe

an old scottish woman next to me tells her
friend "half six in the morning" sounds like
something else to me ya immature i know perhaps
but fuck i haven't half sixed in forever i used to half
six all the time. not so much. anymore. not so much to my
dismay, Now this may sound a bit nonsensical but
please hear me out brown sauce red sauce saucer saucers
clinkity clink teaspoons and such. full scottish on the way get back
to new york get yer cholesterol and yer triglycerides checked milk
steams in the other room and outside plumes of charred ocean rise from
manufacturing grounds coffee grounds here comes the latte i wonder if it's
oat or soy it's oat she says wait it out let it cool let it burn don't burn your mouth
Now the bagpipes come in i swear they do, the winds cool / juxtaposition against
the morning's stagnant warmth square square funeral at the Scotland round church
children beat each other off with terrible tartan a whale in leopard's skin
flannel floral fleece arrangements sticky pudding fills them sit in sit in
wait to be served return outside to drink / drink in the peated air
that peated air that seems to be keeping the demons in my chest
at bay the bay the waves come come crashing into the bay
calming the left end of my brain turning my breathing
into more of a pleasant hobby and less of a dreaded
task. cock sew my heart and bottle my skull drink
coffee until two, whisky until six, eat
langoustines until seven and sleep
until forever or at least until
edinburgh or glasgow or
tallinn or helsinki "you
like everything that's
not good for you" she
says, the old 'half six'
woman she pours
me a cup of tea
instead.

Tallinn

you're the last pagans on earth
adopt me. and
the trees have souls here
—she shouts
they say where are you from,
        where have you been,
                where are you going?
each response equally
different and inspiring
some songs bring the rain
some, the sun
some sustain either

i've got to learn to not look back
    to not turn around
what's ahead   is beautiful
in all it's glorious uncertainty
and i realize that poetry
is a grand catharsis
but music is the grandest of all
(just let someone else make it
                for now)

i fought and we fought and
finally we broke through the rains
                          of occupation
i traveled back to the
fifteenth century to buy love
potion for the waitress and for
the tour guide but they had vanished
        upon my return

                    so, now,
pockets full of marzipan
and chilly skies galore
the night is a pinnacle
the shops are shut
the doors read 'solitude'
fog infects the bell towers

and on my fifth pint i decide
        i can live here
love is getting so expensive

as inflation grows
        —but the rains of occupation—

drip down into the depths
        polluting my sauntering soul

I Recommend Agriculture

for Niyazi

circle gets the grave
for her birthday
continue to spiral while i
elaborate / elaborate
please list your strengths and your
deficiencies
traffic always gives
happiness to me so
  i recommend agriculture
dental hypocrisy
hip-pa-cra-SEE
and hang a clear portrait
a million glass pieces
a large force (or a farce?)
shattered tranquility but in a size seven and a
       half
(please have it wrapped and
       saved as docx)

this is a photo
of an exploded missile
       a mussel
   exploded, in mid air
as you can see
regrets, or entrees: served first (cold)
   abiding by the ruse
that a flood is imminent
a disappointment, inevitable
dog eat dog eat dog; eat dog
and never ever forget
to remember this:

i recommend agriculture

regards,
remorse

(and then there's words too)

Outside and Drunk Screaming at the Constellations

your new high rise
your lonely homely funeral
oh you; vulnerable castle atop
        my dormant volcano
struggling to see that
there is an easier way
                      forward
unlimited faith-based pills
and piles of false births

she's right
it is rotting me
from the inside out
i can see it every morning the liver the lungs my intestines
my heart

looking down /
/ rotting

parallel anarchy breeding these
        blanket absurdities
this glorious solitude
that forces
the hands of time
to move the goddamned journey
                backwards
beginning with
        one
          single step
 one single
   final countdown
one bloody darkened seatbelt
sign

…your move, orion

Bratislava

la vie en rose plays
in the square
through a clarinet or
a violin
patrick says "focus only on the moment
in front of you,
today is still pregnant
       —tomorrow, unborn"
sunlight slowly fades from the rooftops
yellow to cream to pink and to coral
at half seven the clock tower illuminates
citizens roam the streets humming the tune
that infects the air
       from the clarinet or from
       the violin
they smile
friends clink glasses
girls kiss boys kissed
by moonlight
father swings girl round
in circles
girl giggles with dizziness
a feeling i can now relate to on
my fifth glass
of slovakian wine

Havana

if i
can't make
words pretty
then
what's the
point of
living?
when Hemingway
couldn't write
he would
invite friends over
and rehearse his
suicide.
with the barrel
in between his grinning
lips
and his big
      toe
on the trigger
if i can't make
words pretty
then maybe
i should be
with friends

Baltic Jam

yummy toast and
baltic jam the sun
in front, your jupiter
      in retrospect
mars in introspection
into your deflection pour the
coffee coffee nordic blast and
georgian eggs and russian bombs
armenian beer and whatever the fuck
happens in moldova
save ukraine! make it
rain until the sky it bleeds
dry heaves of a heaven that
never actually existed and
the seas they overflow with
aesthetic plastic mercury
   (planet, not the freddie)
which also happens to be in technicolor
the moon's in technicolor electrolytes
    and metrocards
jupiter, in retrospect
      keeping the asteroids at bay

Death Sharp Minor

fires spreading
in six eight time
among these pleasantries please
                  curb your god

chasing the new king's
ransom through darkness
and brine in the key
of death sharp minor

then i looked around

selecting substance from
styles patiently the
violence fed me with fires
and blue boulevards
spreading in six eight time

the consciousness leaked from
                    your heart
into my blackened lungs
and it sang a familiar chorus
of counterfeit rain
-bows and
        razor blade smiles

this could only be the work
of a dog so hateful and
absent and drunk again
beating with fists
against the fragile panes
surrounding your souls

and a reprise returns
slathered in melancholy
flowers bloom from the
dust that still rattles around
my mind like
dominoes in a coffee can

this could only be the work of
                    the suffering

the fools spreading like fire
like silent melodies
in six eight time

James Joyce's Cane

james joyce's cane
        in a glass box
in a room painted blue
        in a faux library
in a town i despise
            in a state i was born
                      in a country i loathe

on a planet i've not quite yet seen

in a porridge of stars
      on a death-laden sun

in a flowerbed of dog piss

           and love-starved ladybugs

his glass box cane
legs in the dirt
    soil
on a dying rock
    in outer space.

Algebra

bottomless = kaleidoscopes

, nevertheless

two + seasonal depression =
          desti / prosti
  -tute

necks in line seven
  back to back wins
    en-countered by *legacy*

if a = crystal communist
then b < £ (you would suppose)
how many times have we counted

losses on one hand
/ failures on the other
  off to the glacial races
       once again.
  so

look forward to:
- sunlight
- autumn
- perfume
- barley

  it's not always maths.

go towards the light and
dive bomb like the stars

go and
burnout at the speed   of life.

Words

catalogue your   divine fears
count pills count
ocean stars and
  plastic bottles
but be warned, you maybe actually
be s l e e p i n g
do you or a loved one
suffer from capitalism?
 i cannot tell you
how much i love
     —words—
…but how one's
     suffering
   dissipates
without them.
   and unfortunately—that is life
      inside the shell
         of a milk bean.

I've Never Been a Poet in Edinburgh

i've never been a poet in Edinburgh
but as i drift along the pubs and
the shops of the grassmarket
the sunshine and the rain collide
with my aging face, simultaneously
and i wonder what's taken me so long
e v e r y place has a story // a prized
memory locked inside a vault
my mind becomes live theater
the apex where i'd meet neil for
a smoke the hotel where i slept with
lily when i was homeless the italian
cafe where i had lunch with a small
group of russian tourists i was guiding
around with a bloody eye haggis-laden
romantic dinners with peachey on my
novel arrival passing out magic flyers with
canadian owen the shop where i bought
my first guitar with lauren and the rain and
the sun continue to crash harmoniously into
my face there's the bow bar where i'd have
whisky for lunch the alley where i met those
gorgeous israeli dancers the spot where derbhaile
walked off as i clutched my chest to keep the pain
inside where it belongs and i would follow the sounds
of the rain-drops smacking stones beyond and past
the girl dressed up like a hurricane eye—tasting
like oysters // drowning in pearls trying to figure out
a way to put it all into words and i believe this is a
fine start.
      i'll get better with age
      like this glass of whisky,
currently burning through
              my fortunate guts.

Halu

this is the land of a thousand hellos
today only echos remain
think back to now, when
we were hunters
of the sky
for patches and sheaves
of indigo and blue
torn between the penultimate
and the ultimate;
a golden sun-filled
sky and
a warm soft body
      upon waking
but here we are
alone and deaf from
the buckshot
or whatever it is
that the ghosts
still manufacture here
one thing i now know
      it certainly isn't
           desire

Pigeon Two (European Version)

fucking pigeons
how they suddenly became images
                      of grace and of beauty

Timeless Junk Of The Soul

I will consume you
try me
with heart and with
fire
and this timeless
junk of the soul
it spins around
my cerebellum
like a pill
on a roulette wheel
what do you
        even mean?
if the stars don't
shine,
then it isn't dark
enough.

my lungs are shriveling,
black with delight
the monkeyshoulder
it saturates
my liver
it spins around the
temporal lobe
like a quarter
        on a glass
                coffee table
your reflection leaves my eyes
blood rushes down my legs
i try to scream
but my tongue
has been split in two
        the clock says nien
        the year is midnight
she says 'oh god yes'
who is this *god* you shout for?
it's time to go home now
click your heels
return to the void
somebody,
anybody,
please…
call me an uber.

II

driver, driver!
Reykjavik!
and step on it!
this is how I
clear my mind
watch me taste her
once again
and die
smiling between
her thighs
brain versus mind
ego and id
art and expiration
a battle to the death
slow, slow suicide
as the salt forms
above my lips
she calls for this 'god' again
…but i'm already gone
the streets smell like
        nothing
like desert rain
like bad scotch
like happy americans
or the boogeyman
my eyelids burn my
feet carry me to the river
your mind pulls me
in the opposite
        direction

fun fact:
the thing about Reykjavik
is you simply cannot
afford to buy anything
worth having
with only coins
the coin currency there
serves only
one purpose
to fill your pockets
so that you're certain
to drown

as you walk
into
the sea.

III

What shall be
my epitaph?
'here lies:
timeless junk of the soul
of the soul, of the body
and of the mind
of M——S——De——:
artist
        drunk
                coward
failure
        beloved by many,
                a few at a time.'

and my father before me:
sucker,
centrist,
master of finding meaning
                in his suffering
benefactor,
where am I going with this…
oh and you,
emperor,
conquerer
philosopher
        barista
                cat-lover,
                      et al.
all that we have in common
is the nothingness
we came from
and the nothingness
that we are all guaranteed
to return to
so maybe,
based on that fact
stop being
such a prick

to your fellow human
being;
an epilogue,
                        now
the feeling returns
to my tongue
my lips covered
in sweat and
other beautiful images
is she sleeping?
maybe she finally
found her god.
i feel at peace as well
i could sleep for
        ten or six hours

or maybe
  it's finally time
      to shut my eyes and

wake up.

New York, Pt I

I was back in
new york city again
where money and time
disappeared at the same
velocity
and you had your choice
of sweltering heat
or of bone-chilling cold
of beer or of tonic wine
of poverty line or of below-poverty line
and the more madness you created
after midnight
the more the they rewarded you
with crippling debt or with
deafening seclusion
dead man on a car horn
times nine million
a train every twenty or
thirty minutes
stacks of bills
as high as the skyscrapers
they come from

the soul is gone
the fire has leaked out
of my eyes and into the gutters
that lie in the shadows
under theoretical stars

       oh i was back in
       new york city again
just unpacking my things and dreaming
of a leisurely jaunt
to euthanasia
and you

The Coda

and then the chorus comes in
and you run alongside strange
new melodies tripping over
electric wires and golden notes
of charcoal and plague
all the while the stoplights
never change red now
frozen in time
at this rate you'll never
get to the bridge
let alone the coda

a museum of firsts
a flight from madrid
to rome
  to guam
my brain explodes
inside of
my skull

tapas
for the flight crew

  this is the last time
no but this time
    i swear
  this is it this time

a raging wildfire
down to a single
candle's flame

then it all goes out

    poof.

at this rate you'll never
get to the bridge

let alone the coda

nothing left to do
    now

      but wait for years

           for the poison
                  for the reigniting
                        power of

            nostalgia.

iii. passion / void

School Of Eyes

I haven't slept since
I was born
headfirst into
        terror and
discount wines
confessions of confessions
the redundancy of guilt
I remember getting into
Bukowski
to impress a woman
        (irony?)

you say you
can dream in kaleidoscopes
what is that like?
to lose a hundred thousand
        teeth or
to be a million naked bodies
in a school of
        only eyes

You Should Probably Date Me

I like coffee
and breezy
twenty three degree
weather
I dislike mutant
viruses
and injustice
and money

I like money
and sex and whisky
in abundant moderation

my perfect first date:
an international airport
a gin and tonic and a lime
a smoking section
a reclining seat with some
extra legroom and some
Dostoevsky to make me laugh
then and a kiss
on the neck with
the smell of
the ocean
and you

nights in nights out
a cozy five hundred year old pub
with outdoor seating (of course)
you're active
I'm funny
you're contagious
I'm recovering
anxious
nauseous
five foot eleven
middle-aged
angry and disappointed with myself

probably allergic
to your cat

The Show Me State

you were red
from head to toe
a beautiful gait
a vanilla type

begging me to lick
every inch
of your body
forever
         and I tried

your lips
like warm jelly
and now i refuse to swallow

you woke me
        bold
invaded my volcano
                bolder
just like that explosion
                fireworks

on adam clayton powell
                      that night

now
you show me around
you show me
show me Harlem
show me 'normalcy'
you show me
your
museum apartment
this is my landline
this is my typewriter
my ukulele
my chia pet
and this is my body
stop painting the universe

                and kiss me
take me now
this is my bed
my art

my pikachu underwear
lie down
now show me
show me your
body
and don't call me baby
                in fact
don't call me at all
just show me
show me over and over
and over
until the 4am
birds begin to sing
then follow the sound
downstairs
and into a cab
its time for you to go
i can show you the door
where you came in a plague
and are leaving
human
          once again

Memorial Day

maybe this year
instead of taking
a moment of
        silence
for the men and
women with
guns who
protect
god knows who
from god knows
what
take a moment
to remember those
who died *by*
the gun;
the hundreds of unarmed
and innocent black men
and women
the thousands of innocent
school children
beautiful civilians
of ukraine yemen syria
all those killed
by the gun
by the way,
over oil.
the oil that
is killing
all of us anyway
it's in our lungs our veins our water so
maybe take a moment
take a breath
take a stand take a vow
stop romanticizing
firearms or
or war or amendments
        or combat or flags

and just enjoy your

    stupid fucking   hot dogs

Confessions of an Anti-Natalist

people making people
the ultimate act
of human selfishness
to create unnecessary
suffering
in a world that bills you
to suffer

April Fools

you taste like spring
is in the air the air which
i have not consumed in
more than a year now but
it's sweet and it's heavy   as fuck
i'm surrounded by the sunset
the pinks, the blues,
the feelings i have learned to keep in check
are now dancing violently, cheerfully
inside my throat it burns of
last night's scotch surrounds
my brain while you slept
on my couch
reading Sedaris
and Kafka
and
i smoke cigarettes
out on the fire
escape
wondering now,
if i could finally
leap off
and fly

Queen Victoria

my lavender sagittarius
surprisingly small
like the mona lisa
but you wouldn't know…
you're such a 'vibe'
xl lips king sized eyes
my instant crush
a perfect segue
into the new
abnormal

look at the date:
seven
        eleven
                twenty-one
maybe we should be drinking
in Las Vegas
but that would be
just too domestic
for vagabonds like us

we watch the night evolve
pink becomes black
vodka, cigarettes
cigarettes to spit
leather becomes skin
hours pass through you like stone

i wake for the third time
glitter laden torso
skull full of frenzy
and i step into the shower
though it pains me
to rinse you from my body

how i pray
to the gods of lust and wander
that our paths cross again
anywhere else

but here

OMFG

brain stop
make no
work doing
please help
stupid stupid
heart

You Wish You Knew George

george is a human you
wish you knew
one of the last
greats
though he sometimes shouts
at yellow cars and
red american dartboards
i've never actually seen it
         happen
he'd give you his last buck
and the soup off his bowl
or donate some chuckles;
leave sweets and chocolates
scattered round the lobby
(i've found nougat in my
jacket pockets from twenty
twenty-one and i know it was him)

george is a human you
wish you knew
because every hour
is happy hour
just as it should be
especially down under
at that dreaded cocktail hole
where women reject me
and the booze bleeds your
bank account   dry
but with george, you just
laugh that shit off
and enjoy the life that's left
(because we know it's end times)
and chain smoke until you're
    d-d-dizzy

sometimes george lives
around the corner
on a page from a book
of some maps of Ireland
where there's proper stout and
smoking trees and
more women who reject me
(but not maureen, we all love

maureen)
sometimes i'll drink here
after the drinks i've had
and here is where i try and
sneak george back some
money for all the candy and
soup he's fed me
by tipping twenty-five or
thirty percent
but it's never enough
and that's ok   too
because george knows how much
the boss-man pays me
so we try and make up for the losses
with private toilets and cheap bourbon
       but what i really crave is
the ides of april
that's when george
falls of his horse
and we begin the drink again
because we know this current
                      version of life
is simply unbearable without it
  it's just not sustainable
and george knows this
but he doesn't let that
bother him enough
to stop doing what he does best;
making that small world
around him
happy as fuck
     in the darkest of times

Le Bowling

you showed up tall
and strong
hellbent on influence
an optimist
with the most beautiful face
i've seen in decades
and i should know
about decades

i meant to tell you now
i remember my last time
it was two thousand and
something or other
i had just had a raging
panic attack
on the eiffel tower

and upon waking
from my xanax coma
they took me for pizza in
montparnasse
and then to a place called
le bowling

it hit like backward jazz
or like tinfoil
everything spinning round
anti-clockwise
until the sixth or seventh
drink kicked in
and i woke up
swimming in a fountain
the point is:
i was happy then
it came in waves
and it still does now
i was happy tonight
you should know
in those moments lost
in your gaze or
the viscous colour of your voice
the familiar parisian sound
of the collision of maple

and resin
or maybe it was just
literally being
in someone else's shoes

but
i was
 actually
    happy.

Achtung!

don't kiss me that way
and don't fall in
this wont end well
i'm like poison
ok maybe not poison
but
i'm like a drug
a severely enjoyable toxic
and illicit substance
oh it feels so good at first
and then good some more
until you take too much
and then too much again
and again until it
destroys you
or it
kills you
stand back
and walk away
i promise you
i'm a losing streak on fire

*A Poet's Critique**

i tossed my
manuscript
on the bed
next to her
she began to
      vomit
without even
reading
one single
word

i suppose
i must be
doing
something
      right

*based on factual events

Going Down

lay back now your spine
down towards the fire
        feet towards god
there's something i haven't
tasted in the longest of moments
            i can't quite put my finger on it
but why would i want to
when it lives between my teeth
what's buried between you
and now twenty thirty forty
minutes pass by your
second third fourth obituary
eight ninth burial
silent / crying like a sage
that thick innocuous   warmth
                      fills the air
rancid like a bouquet
of sweet crooked dreams through
 walls
       over the sheets
the longest of gazes
the loudest of silences
the everlasting pine
the pining forever
the left and the right the grandest greens
        and blues
lay back your spine   now

there's something i haven't
tasted in the longest
       of moments

Teenager

am i a teenager again?
i only ask because
                we are
drinking in the park
from paper cups
we suck down baby wine
excited and awkward
clumsy and new
we hang around shopping malls
and kick through piles
        of leaves
tipsy from the storm
forever at this fountain
where the water has gone dry
i lean in to kiss you
but you tell me you have seen
too many ghosts
                    today

Carousel

i used to be a carousel

        and really, most nights

but now
this city stuffed full and

            overflowing

with rage and with
elbows

everywhere, but

i used to be a carousel i suppose
    perhaps rusted and somewhere

sometime in between peaks
of the last great

      variant

when before that
you'd get on

and you'd get on and you'd get off

and really

            most
            nights.

Three Rings

three rings
one for each night
you spent chipping
away at the ice
round the organ
that pumps my blood
the blood you soon
will spill
onto the ground
before me

three rings
you left behind
one for each name
you've chosen
in advance
for the unborn
future

three rings
one for every
major life catastrophe
that has led me
to you

these rings i will
      keep safe
for if someday
you come back, to me
i can return them
to you
with the
three words
you left
tonight
scattered round my
      brain and
     buried
 in my mouth:

Coke Zero Carbon

say a prayer
for scaffolding
this is the heat
we were warned
about
  you say
new york
is the greatest
      city
so i can safely
      assess
you are
either delusional
      or very very wealthy
but i digress
as this blue sphere
melts like plastic
on the sun
say a prayer
for scaffolding
or for the moon
not made of cheese
      but of ice

Something Happened On The Way To Poland

we had a night

      we had a laugh

well…you're *still* laughing
(i'm still smitten)

so i rush off to the presses
but somehow it feels
appropriate to fit this in
as a last minute addition:
—i want to go to war
against the birds, with you
sweep banknotes from the gutters
with you
drink unicum and shit-talk the goddamned kids
with you
i wanna continue to
co-star in our atomium dreams
so please please
please be free tonight
go and meet the rest of the world
ask all the important questions
ask the really really important questions
because in the morning
and in the morning after that
and after that still
i will be here
trying to decide once again
which corner of the planet
gives me the greatest sense of warmth
and whether or not to listen
to my brain
or to trust
my stupid
stupid
heart

The Bubble

think carefully
you're about to submit   again
to become bland   again
take the job and the
     woman and
wine on the weekends
the w-nines
the consolidation of privacy
but make it interesting

I can fill you with
culture and
obscurities
you can teach me how
to grow up
(but only if I *want*
you to)

the wind blows my
     laces undone
it rages through our skulls at
seventy ninth   and second
the first interruption
since the blitzkrieg
of the buddha machines

your eyes are a house of mirrors
too easy to get lost
in   your lips take me to
somewhere else where
I usually like what I see
death whispers her approval
into my ear and suddenly my
existential crises are reserved
for wednesdays and fridays

  what I'm trying to say is—
     I like you

order another glass of
market price and
run your nails
  through my thinning hair

grab hold of me
        from the inside

Words From the Beehive

hello. I'm outspoken. INFJ. futurist.
I like wine, spin class, the cool side of the pillow.
risk-taker. I want to feed you.
there are three things in life that are important:
vaccinations. mommy of one. and don't waste your time.

I'm determined. I'm not looking for love.
people person. usually in the car. can you show me around?

I'm blindly optimistic.
please be loyal and quote Parks and Rec.
I can play guitar but would also take a bullet for a chocolate cake.
trans. can you handle it? please be tall.
please be compassionate. please be a caffeine junkie, a boxing enthusiast.

I'm moderate.
liberal.
agnostic.
buddhist.
mommy of one.
dog mom. can you handle it? I'd like to show you around.

I'm not on here.
I'm never on here.
anime is horror and outdoor drinks only. I only drink outdoors.
more puppies. more books and puppies.
outside only. absolutely no trump voters.

I have big dreams.
fluent in french. portuguese. and sarcasm.
maybe you can show me around? or let's have wine.
computer science. fitness. still learning english.
please be weird. queer/kink only.

is this weird yet? did I make it weird?
classical clarinetist. fitness sucker. dog mom.
I need a bad ass. I already got a good ass.

not my little girl. LOL. not my kid. not my gun.
I'm an avid music connoisseur. I love all serial killers. and most wine.
not a dog mom. can you handle it?

here to have fun. for now.

not for a long time. here for a good time. no cats.
must love dogs. must love tequila. never no to tacos.
pony travel golf. I live in four countries.

finally, my own personal hell: dessert, america and halloween.
just in it for the good time. try to keep it casual. I'm looking for something serious.
                        my own personal hell.

                    I am currently seeking my own personal hell.

Tonight, I Should Have Been Laughing

i cancelled plans
and stayed at home
              tonight
my head feels heavy
so i tilt my brain
       forward
and slowly the words
form sentences
and they drip down
my cheeks and
into my
jaw
i unclench
my teeth and
those sentences   fall
       down my neck
 pass through my heart
and are then swiftly pumped
up into my arms
and out through my fingers

i have no control
over this process
no 'brakes' as you say
once i sit and tilt my head towards
the keyboard
i can't be stopped
it's like the hearts
you will create
someday
once born
they will work
until
they die

Restart.

        she appeared
        i remember thinking

how beautiful

I don't know how
else to describe the
sensation of pressure
in my lungs
    in my   drink
and there it was;
deep stirrings
a flutter of potential
   a new world
              war

we don't even know why.

Scenes From The Local Cafe

mastering the art
of hanging
by a thread
i trade words
with a watchmaker
who doesn't believe
        that time exists
they challenge his wits and
his humor and his socks
but he doesn't bend
he doesn't break
man of lovable
stone

his friend however
a gravity fighter
traveling at light speed
between bar and floor
always a smile
always fueled by nicotine
        and vertigo
like any great
              superhero

then there's the painter
who collects monopoly
        money
in hopes that someday
it's properly assigned
            a value
and i do believe
in a world of primarily pain and suffering
                          he does deserve this

the shady weed dealers
        the boulder girls
            the exotic dancers and
the shit-faced brutes
who idealize them
and then there's you

you come in last
and leave first

through a warm pocket of my lungs
traveling through space and spine
through past memories
and future broken plans
you lit up the the whole goddamned room

now we raise our glasses to you

   now we drink alone
in the dark.

Matthew DeGroat is a writer and musician, currently based in New York City. His poetry is emotionally bittersweet, poignant and honest and when not writing or performing with his band, LUV DOT GOV, DeGroat can be found vagabonding around Europe, or seeking out his next favorite scotch whisky in a dark and quiet Manhattan pub.

www.ingramcontent.com/pod-product-compliance
Lightning Source LLC
Chambersburg PA
CBHW020337170426
43200CB00006B/418